Narad

The Path

The Path
Copyright : Prisma, Auroville
Author : Narad

First edition 2023

ISBN 978-93-95460-53-8 (Paperpack)
ISBN 978-93-95460-81-1 (ebook)

BISAC Code:
POE000000, POETRY / General
POE009000, POETRY / Asian / General
POE003000, POETRY / Subjects & Themes / Inspirational & Religious

Thema Subject Category:
DC, Poetry
DCF, Poetry by individual poets
D, Biography, Literature and Literary studies
DSC, Literary studies: poetry and poets

Cataloging-in-Publication Data for this title is available from the Library of Congress.

Published by:
PRISMA, an imprint of Digital Media Initiatives
PRISMA, Aurelec / Prayogshala,
Auroville 605101, Tamil Nadu, India
www.prisma.haus

To Sri Aurobindo and Mother for sustaining me in my aspiration to become Their true child and servant of the Divine.

PREFACE

We all have experienced beauty in our lives and many have also known sorrow, but on the path we realize that all we have been through has only been to guide and prompt us to progress. These poems often speak of the challenges we face each day when we make the final and irreversible decision to follow the light. If one or two of these poems resonate with you I will be pleased for they come to me in various moments, times of deep peace, times of inner concentration and in times of stress, but I always feel behind them the grace of Sri Aurobindo pouring through this unworthy soul his gifts. As usual, I take credit only for the errors in reception.

Contents

1. I Sang — 9
2. Beneath Her Blossom-Feet — 10
3. Impediments to Change — 11
4. Sri Aurobindo's Seal — 12
5. In Moments of Stress — 13
6. In Silence and Alone — 14
7. In the Evening — 15
8. In This Enigma — 16
9. Krishna Beloved — 17
10. Look to the Flowers — 18
11. Lord of All the Distant Galaxies — 19
12. Love Undefiled — 20
13. Mother We Implore Thee — 21
14. My Heart of Freedom Sings — 22
15. My Song of Gratitude — 23
16. Nolini — 24
17. O Flame — 25
18. On the Apex of the World — 26
19. On the Day of Thy Departure — 27
20. On the Mother — 28
21. On the Shore of Bengal's Sea — 29
22. Once in Her Presence — 30
23. Our Errant Ways — 31

24. Our Sanctioned Destiny	32
25. Peacock	33
26. Searching	34
27. Secret of Secrets	35
28. Shall We Not Rise Up?	36
29. She Calls My Soul	37
30. Sonnet of Praise	38
31. Speak to Me	39
32. The Anger of the Sea	40
33. The Crown of Evolutionary Years	41
34. What More Is There to Say	42
35. When Visited by Love	43
36. Will We Hold Out?	44
37. Realms We Cannot Know	45
38. Sacred Grail	46
39. Small Room	47
40. Sri Aurobindo, Lift from Me	48
41. The Crossroads	49
42. The Sacred Soil of Auroville	50
43. Warriors	51
44. I Have Known Sorrow	52
45. Among the Offering of Flowers	53
46. Be Grateful – a Poem for B. Sullivan	54
47. I am at Peace	55
48. All Within Her Grace	56
49. In the Singing of the Stars	57
50. A Servant	58

I Sang

I sang upon the hilltops, in the glades,
In forests redolent with earth's perfume
In evening's worship in a simple shrine
And in my room when day was at its close.
I sang in gardens sharing with the flowers
Music of the soil and heard the songs
The singers on the highest boughs return
And met with sages offering my voice
In all its ranges from heights to deepest depths
Until I came to Her and her command,
"You must bring down a music beyond words".
I wrote to Her about my future's work
And She replied in words divine and filled
With love to keep always alive in me
The spirit of consecration and all will be well.
I rarely sing today but the music in my soul
Reaches out in consciousness to all.

Beneath Her Blossom-Feet

I cannot share the pain that clouds her eyes,
The fire raging through the body's walls
Or offer her the weal of Paradise
For each alone must hear the clarion-calls.

Yet humanly we laugh, we cry, we care
And somehow seem to share each other's grief
And having dwelt in love's untainted air
Awhile we walk as one in one belief, —

That every step is seen, each action known
By Him we name as God or Deity,
Through sorrow and joy our souls aware have grown
In birth's unnumbered towards our Destiny.

As conscious beings we again shall meet
And see earth bloom beneath Her blossom-feet.

Impediments to Change

What are the impediments to inner change,
A mind that values reason over all,
Its drama's posture as leader of the world
Assured though it stumbles it will never fall.

A vital aflame with every passing desire
Whose greed and lust exceed both space and time
Its burning need a pestilential fire
Its rise to power a thrill and joy sublime.

Yet most there dwells within his soul the pain
That God-forgetting tortures him at night
Though in the morning he forgets again
That once he knew the brilliance of the light.

Sri Aurobindo's Seal

I met the Lord in his subtle physical home
Crossing a floor of brilliant opaline.
He motioned me towards him saying "come",
Mystical and magical the scene.

Whereon he bade me sit awhile with him,
And touched my chest and entered into me
As the music from a sacred hymn
Reverberates throughout eternity.

Now age has come upon me rapidly
Though when I go within I bow and kneel
To have been blessed by him eternally
The imprimatur, Sri Aurobindo's seal.

In Moments of Stress

In moments of stress when the nerves are frayed
On this merry-go-round of human desires and needs
When the soul of man seems in falsehood arrayed
And bears within the sprouting of evil's seeds.

One insane act could be the end of all,
Perhaps the ultimate catastrophe
When the hardened heart no longer can hear the call
And the blinded eye can no longer see

And the demon walks before us as we go
Strong and joyous at our heart's unease.
The inability within to grow,
But in battles with the ego find surcease

We walk into the Light from which we came
Upon our lips repeating the sacred Name.

In Silence and Alone

Here I stand in silence and alone
Yet not alone for most aware of Thee
Filling my soul with peace and silent joy
Beaming through me the light of eternity.

Can we find in ourselves a gratitude
Sufficient for the Grace that has come down,
A vision of the future's plenitude
And joy through which our earth-born souls have grown.

There is a humility in surrender full and bright
A vastness in the soul that now is free
From mortal constraints whose final destiny
Assured, resolved from mortal entropy.

In the Evening

In the evening in the moonlight
When the sun has said farewell
I speak Her name and in the white
Silence I hear the evening bell

That calls the faithful to the prayer
In rooms of sanctuary and peace,
But I alone in a diviner air
Rest and let the thought-mind cease.

In this sacred atmosphere
Alone I invoke the Grace
Beneficent and drawing near,
Entering the sacred place

Behind the heart and through thin veils,
A place supreme where Mother dwells
And as the Presence never fails
I forget the thorns of human hells

And I become more than the "I",
A portion of divinity.

In This Enigma

In this enigma of life proceeding to death
Where we move unconsciously each day
Living each moment with this frail and shortened breath
Of past, present and future what can we say.

But tread the path of inner discipline
Aspiring to grow into the truth
To feel within ourselves the fire begin
Throwing away the false and the uncouth.

We live our lives less conscious than the stone
And move as automatons through all our days
And in our crowds then are we most alone
To others we look for constant words of praise.

There is little we feel for which we must atone
For ego led we believe that we have grown.

Krishna Beloved

O night bereft of moon the stars shall guide
My steps upon the winding roads of time,
No taint of darkness ultimately can hide
Nor veil from sight the mystery sublime.

I've found the fruited grove where the God-child plays
And slumbers in this hidden cave of mine,
Opening late the secret Book of Days
I befriended Him as I cleansed the vaulted Shrine.

In dream-like fields amongst the golden kine
I spy his blue-white radiance abroad
Fluting to rapturous bloom this earth divine,
Krishna, beloved, friend and guide and Lord.

Look to the Flowers

Look to the flowers and find thy heart's release
Inhale their fragrance and the miracle air
That beauty found on earth shall never cease
For it symbolizes the Mother's perfect care.

Humans too are images of God
But slowly evolve due to ego's hold
Descended to earth upon this sacred sod
And destined to attain the heavenly gold.

Eternal wars within and fierce without
Must cease if man can yet hope to survive
His pride, his greed, no longer can he shout
If he would conquer death and truly live.

Lord of All the Distant Galaxies

Lord of all the distant galaxies
And all the unknown realms of solar space
Importuning Thee I asked to never cease
The transformation of the human race,

That evil and mediocracy may go
And by Thy Grace a greater light appear
Hastening our ability to know
The descending Truth as it comes ever near.

Beauty and bliss the crown of mortal life,
The peace within that bears the hate and pain
Of instrumental forces and the strife
That they inflict shall not for long remain

And the sacrifice for which Thou suffered birth
Shall come, the gift of Life Divine on earth.

Love Undefiled

In this intransigence of ego-self
The psychic being weeps its longing tears
To break free from this overburdening elf,
And prays the clinging vital disappears.

There are realms that They have shown to me
In subtle worlds and solar vastnesses
And taken me to lands of subtlety
Where the kine feed silently on sweetnesses

In realms of beauty to mortal man unknown.
There all perfection is and all a charm
On moonstone floors a majesty is shown
And nothing there of falsehood to cause alarm.

There blue-winged songsters sing among the flowers
In a paradise of supramental light
With golden fountains pouring forth their showers
A world impregnable to the approach of night.

Here love undefiled has found its home
In Mother, Queen of all the worlds beyond
Who invites the fearless traveler to come
And rest from labour on this sacred ground.

Mother We Implore Thee

Mother we implore Thee in these dark
And turbulent days of Covid's disease
Where governments write laws grim and stark,
Ignoring earth's cry, doing as they please

With edicts unjust to satisfy their greed
And power lust, the millions to control,
Such is the ego and its Insatiable need
To thwart the advent of the aspiring soul,

Its harmony, desireless love and peace.
Mother, save the world from darkness' grip
Allow that aspiration shall not cease
Or we in ignorance to evil slip

But work with earth in its evolving way
And halt the evil forces rampant play.

My Heart of Freedom Sings

Battered and broken, a crippled human blot
And know that by the Grace of God go I
And yet I know that within my soul I am not
This lump of clay but all humanity.

The winds caress me and the sun is warm
Yet in my shattered form I am one
Who has suffered by many a violent evil harm
And know that my human journey is far from done.

I came into this world a body whole
But those who bore me mangled every bone
Yet could not touch my strong eternal soul.
Now He is with me though I am alone.

I find my peace among the simple things
And in the silence my heart of freedom sings.

My Song of Gratitude

An infinity of waiting to see His Face
An eternity of calling for the Grace

To transform this erring soul and bring
The Immortal in this house to sing

And all the Gods to come and hear my prayer
With the Lord and Mother Divine seated there,

My song of love, my song of gratitude
Shall not cease, there will be no interlude

But offering of self's humility
As the sand accepts the offer of the sea

And night embraces the splendour of the moon
And earth rejoices at returning noon.

Nolini

I have written a small homage to the one
Who counselor and friend, the Soul I knew,
Nolini of the Ashram, far advanced
Upon the Purna Yoga's challenging path. He
came in the night when I was deep in sleep
Teaching me the lessons I would need
As I ascend towards Her Golden Feet.
His kindness and his care uplifted me
In the early days of Auroville
When I exhausted came into his room
And he recharged me with his loving hands
That I might work again with energy for Her.
He told us once after Mother left
That she had put a part of herself in us!
I bow before his memory with joy
And gratefulness in all my lives to come.

O Flame

O Flame once lit keep growing through these days,
Of latter years when life must fade and die
Let me not forget my stellar hymns of praise
Or the melodic strains of humility.

Thou hast placed in me blessings most divine
And I consecrate remaining years to Thee
You have given me directions and the sign
Of the future's gifts from all eternity.

Let me bow down each day in silent praise
Knowing thou hast come to lift the poor
And in my soul I sing Thy endless Grace
And walk in joy through the open door.

Each moment of my life has become a song
Of worship that shall carry me along.

On the Apex of the World

Standing on the apex of the world
With Mother showing me the galaxies
And seeing all the nebulae that hurled
Across the vasts of space that I might seize,

She said, "I have shown you the multiplicity
That you may realize the unity."

She told me then not to be afraid
For soon my head would fall off, Her words touched me
Muladara!
This is the game that He has played
Throwing himself into infinity.

Can we with all sincerity decide
To take the Golden Path, the higher way
Or in our ignorance still run and hide
In night that shields us from the coming day?

On the Day of Thy Departure

I remember when you spoke to me
In soothing tones melodically
You spoke to me of music's power
Of Chopin and the brilliant shower
Of sound descending through the OM
That now has become my spirit's home,
And how I must bring new music down
In choral sounds the darkness drown
Then you asked me to build the gardens,
And then you left this dark and dense
Beloved earth to which you came.
And I a nothing spoke your name
And will forever aspire to be
Your servant in humility.
For Thou art all and all is Thee
And below Thy Feet eternity.

On the Mother

I touched Her Feet divine and silently
As she pressed the yearning breast of earth,
Her voice filled my spirit with surprise
The intoxicating beauty of her eyes,
Her speech that is the very voice of God
Her touch that healed the voiceless and forlorn
Her laugh a sun spinning through the skies
Her counsel to the illiterate and wise
All this and more to all who felt Her Grace
And placed their head upon Her offered lap
That through Her there might evolve a higher race
To change man's future from a dark demise
And bring on earth the ultimate Beauty's prize,
A race of beings powerful and bright
Who bring to us the Supramental Light.

On the Shore of Bengal's Sea

Standing on the shore of Bengal's sea,
Breathing the air of the Ashram's harmony
I look upon the years that have flown by
Since first I came upon this shore and I
By some unexpected Grace met the Queen,
The Mother of all these souls who have heard the call
From India and far off lands that all
Are welcome to adventure deep within,
Foregoing ritual, device and sin,
The song celestial, the path begin
Forsaking the past and all its vanity
To find within the Peace of sanctity.

Once in Her Presence

Once in her presence I stepped out of time
And meeting her I felt a soul I knew,
But life on earth is a sharp and arduous climb
The days we had together were very few.

How many times alone I think of her,
This gentle radiant goddess on my way
Who blesses me and carries me yet further
To these heights of beauty and a radiant day.

I love her and my silent soul agrees
No taint of darkness dares to interfere
But a vastness comes as of benevolent seas
Her loving voice is all I wish to hear.

Soon she will come and all my pain shall heal
Our love and joy shall be our spirits seal.

Our Errant Ways

Only the material sheath remains
Blessed raiment of the Godhead's gift,
Symbol of the sacrificial gains
For man endured his spirit to uplift.

In this room of mortal life now dwells,
Enlightening, enrapturing our days,
The Presence of the Mother in our cells
Transforming by Her Love our errant ways.

Our Sanctioned Destiny

The OM through all the physical world resounds
And through the planes of higher consciousness
In countryside and metropolis, it sounds,
Awakening and inspiring holiness.

I have sung it on the mountains, by the sea
As threadlike monody or symphonic score,
In waking and in sleep it sings to me
Above the ceiling of mind, below the floor

Of man's unconscient self, his lethargic sleep.
It sings to us of all that we might gain
From true surrender to the Force and keep
Secure in our hearts, relieved from pain

Free from death and its ignominy,
Awake to truth our sanctioned destiny.

Peacock

The peacock calls and his voice resounds
Moving his head in forward jerking starts
Going about his planned diurnal rounds
Moving steadily down from a tree departs

Landing on the soil of earth once more
But when his fan is spread, upon my eyes
I see Krishna dancing as before
When I was there with the Gods in paradise.

Will I see him in his home again
Or walk with him among the gentle kine
Will he appear on earth to earthly men
Will his entrancing flute-song be our sign

Or is he already here and filled with care
We see him not in the resplendent air.

Searching

Searching, searching in all this chaos of mind
For one true moment of a silent peace
To look within the fullness of faith to find
The hidden trigger of the soul's release.

Days and hours and aeons seem to pass
And growth is slow, the inner wars still wend
Their subtle and nefarious ways, alas,
When will the darkness of our beings end.

A guardian angel guides us we are told
Accompanying us through all our lives
Nurturing wayward souls to the fold
Seeing that only the good in us survives.

Secret of Secrets

A secret of secrets fills my heart today.
Words fail me as I look into her eyes
Truly there is nothing more to say
Of this gift to me this true divine surprise.

Her name repeats within my peaceful mind
I image her as once I held her close,
Her generosity is of a higher kind,
Scent of the jasmine, perfection of the rose.

Child of the vaulted heavens and of this life,
Return to my arms, beloved over all,
For us there is in love no pain or strife
Together we have heard the Eternal's call.

Shall We Not Rise Up?

Bitterness and enmity are not the way
There is in man the possibility
To recognize upon this earth the play
Of beings inimical who live to see

The darkness rule our erring lives and then
Restrain the evolutionary force
Reverting man to animal again
Directing life towards a lowly course.

What then of those bright souls who came to save,
Their words still burning on ethereal pages
And all the love and beauty and peace they gave.
Our denial of the truth brought down by sages,

The work of avatars and holy men laid waste
Their untiring work to uplift transform and save,
Forgotten the holocaust, the pain they faced
As man in his lust and greed wends to his grave.

There is in all a being filled with light,
A love so strong no demon can attack
Shall we not rise up and face enveloping night
Against suppression of the Truth fight back?

She Calls My Soul

Here in Madhuca my daughter's home
I have returned to blossom in Aurovillle
No more those welcoming continents to roam.
Of this world's gifts I have had my fill.

In these evening years I dwell in this blessed land
And tend within the flame burning all the years
Of beauty found and love's most gentle hand,
When Death tore her from me and the human tears

Flowed copiously until in Mother's care
I rested and replenished life and soul.
Working in the Garden's special air
I am aware of the moment and the goal,

For here the ego self must abdicate
And the shining of the soul come through
My time on earth is brief, I cannot wait
My soul must rise and be born anew.

We must bring the integral harmony to men
Opening them to Her love and Grace again.

Sonnet of Praise

Of all the grandeur in the world I've seen
There is no bliss or beauty to compare
With the awakening of Auroville's green
Forests and her miracle of air.

The world appears to darken with deceit
And lands once fertile now are sterile fields
Polluted beneath the workers wounded feet
And poisoned water a toxic harvest yields,

But there is hope, humanity assured
That an evolutionary race with come,
Malignant forces that once had seemed inured
To evil made scented earth their home

Shall pass as dust borne by a solar wind
And God his love to human hearts shall bind.

Speak to Me

Speak to me so sweetly of Thy Name
And all my soul shall bend and touch Thy Feet,
I bow before Thee importunate and lame,
Mother, who I've been graced by love to meet.

The years have flown, yet ever young I find
My spirit yearning urgently to be free
From repetiveness of vital life and mind
And surrender self in freedom's joy to Thee.

This world of pain and woe must disappear
Replaced by Bliss, the angels of the bright
Power and the beauty drawing near,
The dawning of the Supramental light.

May man awake and lean into the day
With folded hands in gratitude to pray.

The Anger of the Sea

Once I felt the anger of the sea.
It seemed to laugh as it accosted me
Hurling its waves upon the lonely shore
Battering the beach with impunity.

I walked the sand and felt a numbing fear
Of rushing beauty suddenly gone wild
Yet knew I was protected in the way
That God protects his lonely errant child

From all the haunting dangers he will face,
Whose hidden self takes refuge in Her smile
And in His hands that save, the love that guides
The seeking soul from stealthy Evil's guile.

I left the sea and all the earth behind
My soul, my truth within, my Lord to find.

The Crown of Evolutionary Years

Now the peace that earth longs for begins
For descending from the heights there has come down
Upon a sanctified world now free of sins,
The beauty of a love divine, the crown

Of all these evolutionary years
Since mind appeared in human history
And man has wept his hundred million tears
And cried in desperation to be free.

What More Is There to Say

What more is there to say,
Souls in sorrow weep
Shattered hearts replay
The hour of death to keep

Alive the dying face
Beloved of all things.
Remembrance is a grace
To which our being clings

Until we realize
The soul in us that knows
Nothing ever dies,
To life there is no close

And we must carry on,
The need for death explore
Until the work is done
And God is found once more.

When Visited by Love

When we no longer carry ego's shield
Or halberd of our insignificant thought
And see in others enemies to yield
On bloodstained fields in senseless battles fought,

When we no longer need the taste of tears
And open to the wonder of it all,
God from our shadowed background reappears
Responding to the spirit's urgent call.

Then shall we truly wake and realize
The One who in each living creature dwells,
Who looks on us with calm compassionate eyes
As light divine invades our human cells.

The lotus from the mire blooms above,
So too our lives when visited by love.

Will We Hold Out?

Will we hold out against the evil's thrust
Or fall and in a desperate failing chance
Finally accept the offer of the Grace.
Or is sedentary man too satisfied
With his minute kingdom now established here
To take the leap and on the precipice
Walk into the sunlight of Her smile?
I know that all creation moves towards Thee,
The cycles turning upward see Thy Face,
O Mother, O creatrix, guide our steps
And would that we be willingly free.
May that hour dawn O Lord of Peace,
May the evil of this world finally cease.

January 2, 2022

Realms We Cannot Know

And there were strawberries, currants, grapes and more
And one could move in silence through the corn.
The garden was a child's delightful store
And special was the waking in the morn

When one could feast upon the beauty of the earth.
My father planted a banquet for each child.
I remember him and all his moments of mirth
Who understood his children could be wild

But nurtured them with a strong yet silent love.
The house was small but fitted to our size,
A treasure trove where we could safely move
And our mother's dishes were the greatest prize!

They are gone now to realms we cannot know
And eventually in joy I too shall go.

March 13, 2022

Sacred Grail

A great stress has come upon Auroville
And pain the dark companion of an hour,
Intolerance, misunderstanding spill
Across the fabric of peace and tend to lower
The consciousness and hope for unity.
When will the collective harmony begin,
Or will the ego rule and the disparity
Widen among her children and the din
Of anger and hostility override
The evolutionary thrust, the Grace
Descending, from which we cannot possibly hide,
For willingly we came to this sacred place.
I know this city well, it cannot fail
And the Matrimandir is its sacred grail.

March 7, 2022

Small Room

Alone I sit in my small room of peace
Away for a time from all this life's discord
Where the violence of the world seems to cease
And I am close to Mother and the Lord.

How many years remain I do not know,
I once was ageless but perfidy and lust
Of one I loved has truly laid me low
And fled from us the element of trust.

Truly at the end we go alone
To the place of peace and calm where we shall rest
Until we take another birth or none
Forgetting self, forgetting love, at best

The human love that stabs the soul with pain
Until we rise purified of stain.

Sri Aurobindo, Lift from Me

Sri Aurobindo lift from me this pain,
Its knife of infamy cutting through my soul
A rapid thrust and all comes back again,
Her falsehood, treachery, deceit and all.

The days and hours I lived with her unknowing
The darkened path she took that brings such grief,
A sorrow as when winter winnowing
The final flower the last remaining leaf.

Will I as man be able to overcome
The treachery and the abuse of love
That has settled in my heart as in its home
By some greater dispensation from above?

Or is all lost and I am fortune's fool
Having loved in vain and now dark Nature's tool?

The Crossroads

Standing at the crossroads of a race
When evil seems to hold the higher ground
And yet a movement feel that will replace
This errant life and ultimately found

The gnostic being rising out of man
Where love and power silently appear
To create a new world following a plan
The Divine has sanctioned through His self-born seer

Of all the ages, the two who lead the way,
Sri Aurobindo and Mother, the avatars
Who have taught us how to live and how to pray
For release from all that in us mars

The advent of the Supramental Force,
For nothing can halt its Truth or slow its course.

March 13, 2022

The Sacred Soil of Auroville

I have reentered the soil of Auroville
Behind me stands the sacred Matrimandir
Beside me the plants are calling to me still,
"Transplant us to the Gardens atmosphere".

Long have we languished waiting for the day
We She will see us in our perfect form
In the gardens where all the gods can play
When the impossible becomes the norm.

I have vowed to honor their silent prayer
With tender love to aspire and create
The ideal atmosphere in scented air
For all mankind to meet and meditate.

The hour has come, the call is ringing clear
To proceed with care and garden without fear.

Warriors

Still am I now in this sanctuary of peace
And long have I aspired to become
A soul devoted to Them and to release
The karma of the growth of a small child.
The hour is upon us we must not wait
While the whirling of the world seems wild,
Distorted and the Truth supreme, divorced.
There is a hand uplifting all to Light
Yet evil's touch on humanity has forced
This separation and our mortal plight.
Can we in collective harmony unite
As warriors in evolution's fight?

March 13, 2022

I Have Known Sorrow

I have known sorrow heavy as a stone
And grief and pain in years when most alone,
Bur One came down and harboured in my breast
Allowing me deep comfort, peace and rest.
He remains today, a silent welcome Guest
And guide upon my path that I not fail
In the mystic journey on which I have set sail.
The gentle Lady with the knowing eyes
Has also come from realms beyond the stars
To tend my soul, and the slowly healing scars
And send the clouds of darkness to their demise.

Among the Offering of Flowers

Let all be honest and admit
We let the hostile forces in
They come with scintillating wit
Inviting us to share their sin.

And though we hold in sanctity
In our secret heart the rose
Their darkness of such profundity
Holds us to their congress close.

And then we pray for Her relief
From evil beings entering
Trying to shake us from belief
With their nearly fatal sting.

We breathe again in restful hours
The atmosphere of calm and peace
Among the offering of flowers
And find in Love our soul's release.

Be Grateful – a Poem for B. Sullivan

Be grateful for the constant gifts of life,
A blazing sunrise never seen before
Three owls siting on a sacred tree,
A silent walk upon a lonely shore,

A heron winging silently at dawn
A nestling warbler singing his first song
A perfect flower in a pathless wood,
A music in the heart that lingers long,

The morning faces of the very young,
The easy wisdom of the very old,
The summer ending with its fiery touch
The frigid welcome of the winter's cold.

Hold each moment precious in the soul
Forgetting not the journey and the goal.

I am at Peace

I am at peace and my deep soul
Would offer all my life to Thee
The body, mind, emotions, all
As offering thy slave to be.

All Within Her Grace

All the beauty of the world I've seen
Cannot compare with that she gives to man
The briefest glance from her we might nigh deem
A blessing as she passed by in her van.

And when she spoke the angels silent fell
Listening to her words that carried all
The worlds, the cosmos and more than one could tell
But felt the impact in the very soul.

And when she looked in a disciple's eyes,
The radiance that penetrated mind
And body, as if taken by surprise
A silence fell on the anointed kind.

Here in the Ashram all within her Grace
Felt the inception of an eternal race.

2020

In the Singing of the Stars

In the singing of the stars I homage thee,
In the rivers of the world thy forces flow
In the flower's fragrance thou anointest me
And lesson me in all that I must know.

On the mountain top I sought for Thee
Long I searched for Light and could not find
Then one day recognized thou art in me,
Above my flaws, above my limited mind

And now, aware of all that I must do,
Surrender, offering, sincerity,
To calm the mind and vital to come to you
And live in you for all eternity.

2021

A Servant

I found him in the strangest place,
Hidden beneath the moss and stone
And in his hands the heavenly Grace
Meant for those who feel most alone,

Who are not controlled by the seething masses
Intent on gaining their portion of wealth
Vying with the upper classes
Oft to the detriment of their health.

One called me from a far-off land
That I somehow knew as my spirit's home,
Where my soul must take its final stand
To turn to Light, no more to roam.

The body ages but the Grace
Ever present steadies me
In this vast world to know my place,
A servant of Divinity.

June 17, 2021

International Publications

Auroville Architecture
by Franz Fassbender

Auroville Form Style and Design
by Franz Fassbender

Landscapes and Gardens of Auroville
by Franz Fassbender

Inauguration of Auroville
by Franz Fassbender

Auroville in a Nutshell
by Tim Wrey

Death doesn't exist
The Mother on Death, Sri Aurobindo on Rebirth
Compiled by Franz Fassbender

Divine Love
Compiled by Franz Fassbender

Five Dream
by Sri Aurobindo

A Vision
Compiled by Franz Fassbender

Passage to More than India
by Dick Batstone

The Mother on Japan
Compiled by Franz Fassbender

Children of Change: A Spiritual Pilgrimage
by Amrit (Howard Shoji Iriyama)

Memories of Auroville - told by early Aurovilians
by Janet Feran

The Journeying Years
by Dianna Bowler

Auroville Reflected
by Bindu Mohanty

Finding the Psychic Being
by Loretta Shartsis

The Teachings of Flowers
The Life and Work of the Mother of the Sri Aurobindo Ashram
by Loretta Shartsis

The Supramental Transformation
by Loretta Shartsis

The Mother's Yoga - 1956-1973 (English & French)
Vol. 1, 1956-1967 & Vol. 2, 1968-1973
by Loretta Shartsis

Antithesis of Yoga
by Jocelyn Janaka

Bougainvilleas PROTECTION
by Narad (Richard Eggenberger), Nilisha Mehta

Crossroad The New Humanity
by Paulette Hadnagy

Die Praxis Des Integralen Yoga
by M. P. Pandit

The Way of the Sunlit Path
by William Sullivan

Wildlife great and small of India's Coromandel
by Tim Wrey

A New Education With A Soul
by Marguerite Smithwhite

Featured Titles

Divine Love

The texts presented in this book are selected from the Mother and Sri Aurobindo.
"Awakened to the meaning of my heart. That to feel love and oneness is to live. And this the magic of our golden change, is all the truth I know or seek, O sage."

Sri Aurobindo, Savitri, Book XII, Epilog

A Vision by the Mother

On 28th May 1958, the Mother recounted a vision she once had of a wonderful Being of Love and Consciousness, emanated from the Supreme Origin and projected directly into the Inconscient so that the creation would gradually awaken to the Supramental Consciousness. The Mother's account of this vision was brought out a first time in November 1906, in the Revue Cosmique, a monthly review published in Paris.

A Dream – Aims and Ideals of Auroville
the Mother on Auroville

50 years of Auroville from 28.02.1968 - 28.02.2018
Today, information about Auroville is abundant. Many people try to make meaning out of Auroville – about its conception, to what direction should we grow towards, and, what are we doing here?

But what was Mother's original Dream and what was her Vision for Auroville back then?

Matrimandir Talks by the Mother

This book presents most of Mother's Matrimandir talks, including how she conceived the idea for this special concentration and meditation building in Auroville.

Memories of Auroville - Told by early Aurovilians

Memories of Auroville is a book about the very early days of Auroville based on interviews made in 1997 with Aurovilians who lived here between 1968 and 1973. The interviews presented in this book are part of a history program for newcomers that I had created with my friend, Philip Melville in 1997. The plan was to divide Auroville's history into different eras and then interview Aurovilians according to their area of knowledge.
Our first section would cover the years from 1968 till 1973 when the Mother was still in her physical body.

The Way of the Sunlit Path

May The Way of the Sunlit Path be a convenient guide for activating this ancient truth as a support for a Conscious Evolution.
May it illumine the transformation offered to us in the Integral Yoga.

A Dream Takes Shape (in English, French, Hindi)

A comprehensive brochure on the international township of Auroville in, ranging from its Charter and "Why Auroville?" to the plan of the township, the central Matrimandir, the national pavilions and residences, to working groups, the economy, making visits, how to join, its relationship to the Sri Aurobindo Ashram, and its key role in the future of the world. This brochure endeavours to highlight how The Mother envisioned Auroville from its inception, some of the major achievements realised over the years, and some of the difficulties currently faced in implementing the guidelines which she gave.

Mother on Japan

I had everything to learn in Japan. For four years, from an artistic point of view, I lived from wonder to wonder. And everything in this city, in this country, from beginning to end, gives you the impression of impermanence, of the unexpected, the exceptional... ...everything in this city, in this country, from beginning to end, gives you the impression of impermanence, of the unexpected, the exceptional. You always come to things you did not expect; you want to find them again and they are lost – they have made something else which is equally charming.

Auroville Reflected

On 28 February 1968, on an impoverished plateau on the Coromandel Coast of South India, about 4,000 people from around the world gathered for a most unusual inauguration. Handfuls of soil from the countries of the world were mixed together as a symbol of human unity. Why did Indira Gandhi, the erstwhile Prime Minister of India, support this development for "a city the earth needs?" Why did UNESCO endorse this project? Why does the Dalai Lama continue to be involved in the project? What led anthropologist Margaret Mead to insist that records must be kept of its progress? Why did both historian William Irwin Thompson and United Nations representative Robert Muller note that this social experiment may be a breakthrough for humanity even as critics commented, "it is an impossible dream"?

A House For the Third Millennium
Essays on Matrimandir

Nightwatch at the Matrimandir...
A cosmic spectacle; the black expanse above, the big black crater of Matrimandir's excavation carved deep into the soil. The four pillars - two of which are completed and the other two nearing completion - are four huge ships coming together from the four corners of the earth to meet at this pro propitious spot...

Passage to More than India

This book is a voyage of discovery. In 1959 the author, Dick Batstone, a classically educated bookseller in England, with a Christian background, comes across a life of the great Indian polymath Sri Aurobindo, though a series of apparently fortuitous circumstances. A meeting in Durham, England, leads him to a determination to get to the Sri Aurobindo Ashram in Pondicherry, a former French territory south of Madras.

www.ingramcontent.com/pod-product-compliance
Lightning Source LLC
LaVergne TN
LVHW010434070526
838199LV00066B/6024